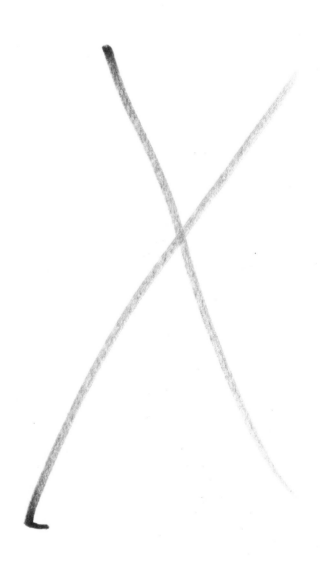

Straight to the Source

Primary and Secondary Sources

John Hamilton

ABDO
Publishing Company

visit us at
www.abdopub.com

Published by ABDO Publishing Company, 4940 Viking Drive, Edina, Minnesota 55435.
Copyright © 2005 by Abdo Consulting Group, Inc. International copyrights reserved in all
countries. No part of this book may be reproduced in any form without written permission from
the publisher. The Checkerboard Library™ is a trademark and logo of ABDO Publishing
Company.

Printed in the United States.

Cover Photo: Corbis
Interior Photos: Corbis pp. 1, 5, 7, 8, 9, 11, 12, 15, 17, 20, 22, 25, 27; Library of Congress p. 7

Series Coordinator: Stephanie Hedlund
Editors: Kate A. Conley, Jennifer R. Krueger
Art Direction: Neil Klinepier

Library of Congress Cataloging-in-Publication Data

Hamilton, John, 1959-
    Primary and secondary sources / John Hamilton.
        p. cm. -- (Straight to the source)
    Includes index.
    Summary: Discusses the process of writing a research paper and the difference between
primary and secondary source materials and how to evaluate them.
    ISBN 1-59197-548-4
    1. Report writing--Juvenile literature. 2. Research--Methodology--Juvenile literature. [1.
Report writing. 2. Research--Methodology.] I. Title.

LB1047.3.H36 2004
372.13028'1--dc22
                                                            2003055831

Contents

Research Papers

As a student, you will have to write many kinds of papers. One kind is an essay, where you write about your opinion. Another is a research paper, where you support your opinion with facts.

A well-done research paper is full of information. To find this information, you will have to look at many different facts. They can be found in primary and secondary sources.

A primary source is an actual record that has survived from the past. A secondary source is a record that was created some time after an event. So, it is one or more steps removed from the original event.

Most research papers include information from both primary and secondary sources. Your task is to find the right kind of each. Then, you must combine your research with your own ideas.

Opposite page: *Research papers help students solve problems or change others' minds about a subject.*

Primary Sources

When writing a research paper, you want to learn as much as possible about your subject. One way to do that is to study primary sources.

A primary source is the result of firsthand knowledge of a topic. So, it is often the best way to get close to an event or subject.

There are many types of primary sources. Some are created by a person who actually witnessed an event. These sources can be **memoirs** or diaries. They are written accounts of a person's thoughts and observations.

EXTRA!

Examples of Primary Source Materials

★ Manuscripts, speeches, interviews, letters, memos, or diaries
★ Autobiographies
★ Photographs
★ Artifacts or personal belongings
★ News programs
★ Official documents including birth and death records, marriage licenses, or census reports
★ Maps and charts

Opposite page: *The original copies of Anne Frank's diary, "The Star-Spangled Banner," a map by John C. Frémont, and a marriage license are examples of primary sources.*

A photograph is also a primary source. It can be used to describe an event. Firsthand investigations such as **surveys**, interviews, and scientific experiments are primary sources, too.

Sometimes, finding primary source materials can be challenging. However, many are located in the library. A librarian can help you find them.

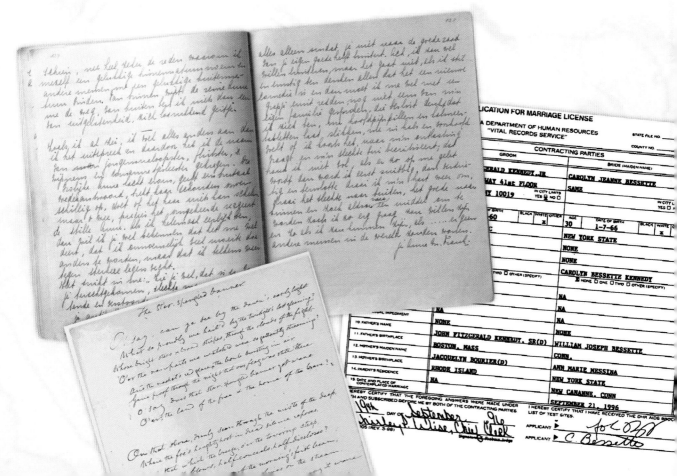

Secondary Sources

Another way to learn about a research topic is to study secondary sources. A secondary source is research that someone else has already done on a subject. It is one step further away from an event than a primary source.

A well-written nonfiction book can be a great source of information.

When using secondary sources, you are relying on an expert's conclusions about your topic. These experts look at accounts of the past that were created by other people. Then, the experts write about the accounts.

There are several types of secondary sources. One is an encyclopedia article. It gives a short, up-to-date summary of a topic. Another is a nonfiction book, which can provide historical background of an event.

A magazine or newspaper article can also provide a good summary of your subject. An article is generally considered a primary source. But, if it is written long after an event, it is a secondary source.

Secondary sources are usually easier to find than primary sources. However, their information may be **inaccurate** or incomplete. So, it is important not to rely only on secondary sources for your research.

Magazine articles can provide research information.

EXTRA!

Secondary Source Uses

Primary sources should be your first choice when doing research. However, secondary sources are also very useful.

Secondary sources introduce a topic. They also provide historical background. And, secondary sources can let you know how historians have interpreted an event.

Finally, secondary sources provide ideas for where to find primary sources. Works cited lists in secondary sources can point a researcher in the right direction.

Evaluation

Finding **accurate** source information to support your paper is important. Unfortunately, not all sources are good. Some source materials may reflect one-sided opinions. The information in others may be incomplete. Some may even be **deliberately** false.

It's your job to **evaluate** the quality of your sources. There are several steps in the evaluation process. First, read your sources critically. Always think about why the material was produced.

For example, when using a diary ask yourself if it was meant to be private. Some **memoirs** are written specifically for publication. So, material may be **exaggerated** or made up. A better source may be one where the author had nothing to gain by writing it.

Next, decide how your sources are biased. Being biased means that a source leans toward a certain point of view. All sources are biased. So, think about who created the material and what bias they may have.

For example, historians are very **skeptical** of eyewitness accounts. Two eyewitnesses can tell two very different stories about the same event. They often miss important details. And, their reports are colored by their own preferences and **prejudices**.

Evaluating sources is an important part of the research process.

The next step is to use the time and place rule. It says a primary source created very close to an event is more **accurate**. So, think about when and where a source was written.

For example, imagine you are writing about a speech. An eyewitness letter written on the day of the speech is likely to be a good primary source. However, an eyewitness account given several years later may be clouded by the passage of time.

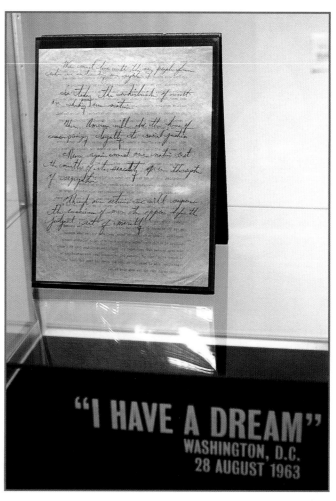

An eyewitness may be a good source for the content of a speech. However, the actual text is a better source.

Finally, check the **accuracy** of a source by cross-checking it against other materials. Sometimes, you can find two or more sources that contain the same information. This means your source is more likely to be accurate.

Evaluating a source will help you separate fact from fiction. It may help to ask yourself the five Ws. They are who, what, when, where, and why. These questions will help you evaluate the quality of your sources.

Questions to Ask When Evaluating a Source

- *Who wrote the source, an expert or an eyewitness?*

- *What is the source trying to do? Is the writer neutral about an event, or does he or she have a reason to tell the story in a certain way?*

- *When did the event occur? How much time passed before the source was written?*

- *Where was the writer of the source? Did he or she actually witness an event, or just record what other people said happened?*

- *Why was the source made? Was it made to make a profit or for personal use?*

Writing Process

Now that you know what sources are available, you can start your research paper. The first step is to select a topic. It can be almost anything. Sometimes your teacher will tell you what to write about. Other times you can choose a topic yourself.

If you get to choose a topic, find one that interests you. If you know something about your topic, it will make your research easier.

The topic you choose will be partly determined by the paper's length. For a short paper, make sure your topic isn't too general. Birds is too broad of a topic for a three-page paper. But narrowing your topic to eagles may be just right.

After you pick a topic, your next step is to write a thesis. It is a sentence that describes what you are trying to accomplish with your paper. It also tells the reader what argument you are making about your topic.

Narrowing your topic will help you develop a thesis. A strong thesis statement will help you focus your paper.

Research papers answer a question or present a point of view. So ask yourself what you are trying to say. Then answer your question to create your thesis.

Before you finish defining your thesis, do some basic research. Checking a general source, such as an encyclopedia, will help you narrow your topic. Selecting a thesis will then be easier.

During your research, you may find a point of view that **contradicts** your thesis. This is called an antithesis. In your research paper, try to find an antithesis to your thesis. Be sure to research this point of view also.

Good research papers address different points of view, even if they go against the thesis. So, don't avoid contradictory information.

Instead, use your research to support your argument. Present the facts, argue your position, and let the readers make up their own minds. When you write a good paper, the readers will see things from your point of view.

Tips for a Strong Thesis

1. Take a stand by showing your conclusions.

2. Justify a need for discussion by showing your topic is controversial.

3. Express only one idea so your paper stays focused and your reader knows what that focus is.

4. Be specific. A thesis should narrow your subject and identify the reasoning behind your argument.

"Eagles help the environment" is a weak thesis. It does not take a stand and is very broad. A stronger thesis is, "Eagles are an important part of the ecosystem, and they should be protected from poachers." This is a controversial argument that you can successfully support with facts.

Outlines

Once you have a thesis, you can make a working outline. An outline labels the parts of your paper that are related. This helps you stay organized. It also helps you focus on what research you need to do.

A working outline changes as you research. Items are altered, added, or dropped as you discover and **evaluate** sources. The outline helps you identify areas where you need more research.

When your research is finished, you will develop a final outline. A final outline will help you write your paper.

Final outlines may be written in fragments or full sentences. This will help you with the flow of your paper. It will also act as a guide for where to insert facts. For these reasons, teachers sometimes require a final outline before you write your paper.

In an outline, Roman numerals show your main ideas.

From there, your outline continues to get more specific. Capital letters show subsections of your main idea.

Then, use numbers to describe details about the subsection.

Finally, show what details are included with lowercase letters.

Eagle Outline

I. Introduction
II. The eagle's role in the ecosystem
   A. Population control
      1. Eats agricultural pests
         a. rodents
         b. rabbits
         c. insects
      2. Eats predators of farm animals
      3. Some say eagles harm ecosystem
   B. Indicates problem in ecosystem
III. Poachers' desire for eagles
   A. Want feathers
      1. for decoration of clothing
      2. for study of migration and evolution
   B. Want specimens for zoos
IV. Conclusion

The first capital letter in your outline suggests that you have more than one idea to support your argument. So, if you have a subsection A, you must also have a subsection B. The same is true for the numbers that describe each subsection's details. If you have a detail number 1, you must also have a detail number 2.

Finding Info

You have a topic, a thesis, and an outline. Now you have to find facts to support your opinion. Finding information for a research paper is like being a detective. Often, you must use creative thinking.

First, ask yourself who might be an expert on your topic. You may find that these people are happy to talk to you. They might also help you find other good primary sources.

An interview is a great way to get information. And, it can help you find other good sources.

Ways to Find Sources

Libraries often have collections of research papers on file. For example, papers that students write to get a master's or PhD degree are often archived by college libraries.

Many libraries and museums have original historical maps, often in digital form. Newsreels that ran in theaters long ago can also be found in libraries and some museums. The Census Catalog & Guide lists many kinds of census data. A librarian will be able to find it for you, as well as other official documents.

Web sites that specialize in government documents can be very helpful in tracking down sources. Often, digital archives of historical photographs are available on the Internet as well.

Another great place to look for sources is a library. Its materials have been sorted and organized to help you find what you need. Libraries also have access to **databases** that show you how to find sources on your topic.

Thousands of books and magazines are written each year about almost any subject. Many books and **periodicals** can be found at the library. Most can be checked out and read at home.

Sometimes libraries even carry materials that haven't been published. These may be collections of private letters, **manuscripts**, and diaries. Most libraries also have CDs, DVDs, video tapes, and audio tapes available. These are all great sources.

Another way to find primary sources is to check the Works Cited page in secondary sources. Some books also list illustration and photo credits. These might point you in the right direction.

The **Internet** can also be a good place to find sources. However, it often has too much information. And, there are many sources on the Internet that are **inaccurate**. So, you have to sift through and **evaluate** the data to find the facts you need.

Your most valuable tool when researching is a librarian. Librarians are trained to find the right sources for your research paper. Be sure to ask for their help.

Opposite page: *Librarians have great ideas for where to find sources.*

Plagiarism

When you write your research paper, use both primary and secondary sources. But write your paper in your own words. If you copy someone else's work, it is a type of cheating called plagiarism.

The Latin root word for plagiarism is *plagiarius*. It means "kidnapper." When you plagiarize, you are stealing. Never use someone else's words or ideas without giving him or her credit. Giving credit is called citing sources.

Schools are strict with plagiarists. You could fail a class for plagiarizing. Some college students may be **expelled**. If you're a reporter, you could be fired. It is difficult for a person accused of plagiarism to repair the damage done to his or her reputation.

Plagiarism is often unintentional. Avoid it by taking careful notes. Always keep track of where your information came from. If you copy a sentence word for word and forget to cite your source, it is plagiarism.

Avoid plagiarizing by putting your sources' ideas into your own words. This is called paraphrasing. However, you should still acknowledge the person who came up with the original idea.

Buying papers on the Internet is also a form of plagiarism.

Citing Sources

To avoid plagiarism and to direct others to your source material, always give credit to your sources. There are several styles for noting sources. One of the most common for research papers is MLA style.

According to MLA, there are two kinds of citations in your research papers. One is **parenthetical** notation. The other is the Works Cited page.

Parenthetical notation identifies a source right in the text of your paper. Armed with this knowledge, the reader can then turn to the Works Cited page.

The Works Cited page is a list of sources at the end of a research paper. There, readers can look up the source in an alphabetical listing. This list gives more details about the source.

The way you cite a source at the end of your paper depends on the sources you include. The *MLA Handbook for Writers of Research Papers* lists methods for many of them. A librarian will also be happy to help you.

Citing your sources is just one part of a well-researched paper. Developing a topic, writing a strong thesis, and finding primary and secondary sources are all important, too. Armed with these skills, you'll be ready to tackle your next research paper!

With hard work and imagination, you can write an A+ paper, too!

Sample Paper

This excerpt from a sample paper shows how a research paper should look. It includes examples of parenthetical notation and entries from the Works Cited page.

Protect Our Eagle Population

The eagle is a bird of prey. It is a beautiful but deadly animal. In fact, eagles are at the top of the food web (National par. 14). So, eagles are an important part of the ecosystem, and they should be protected from poachers.

An ecosystem is an area of land and its living and nonliving parts, such as a forest ("Ecology"). In an ecosystem, the living and nonliving parts affect each other ("Ecology"). An animal at the top of the food chain, like the eagle, is an important part of an ecosystem.

The eagle has many roles in its ecosystem. One is to help control the population of animals that destroy agricultural products. Eagles eat rodents, rabbits, and insects that harm crops (Brown 145). They also eat other animals that attack livestock, such as foxes (Brown 144). So, eagles help farmers by keeping their plants and animals from being harmed.

Many people argue that eagles also attack livestock and game birds, so they are harmful. However, Leslie Brown writes, "No bird of prey is known which feeds exclusively on domestic stock, large or small, or on managed game animals, birds or fish" (143-44). So, these birds will not negatively affect their ecosystem by destroying a large number of farm animals.

Another role of the eagle in its ecosystem is being an indicator. The National Park Service says that the absence of eagles suggests an unhealthy ecosystem (National par. 14). This is because eagles do not have any natural predators (Zoological). Eagles die from old age, human causes, or contaminated food (Jones). If there are no eagles, there is a problem, such as pesticide use, that is affecting their food. This helps the U.S. Fish and Wildlife Service know that there is something wrong.

Works Cited

Brown, Leslie. Eagles, Hawks, and Falcons of the World.
   New York: McGraw, 1968.

"Ecology." The Encyclopedia Americana. 2001 ed.

Endangered Species Act of 1973. Pub. L. 93-205.
   28 December 1973. Stat. 884

Jones, Jim. Personal Interview. 16 February 2004.

National Park Service. 2004. Kenai Fjord National Park.
   16 February 2004.   <http://www.nps.gov/kefj/
Ecosystem/EEagles.htm - Kenai Fjord National Park>.

Zoological Society of San Diego. 2004. San Diego Zoo.
   16 February 2004.   <http://www.sandiegozoo.org>.

MLA style is often used for citing sources. For a book with a single author, MLA has the author's full name followed by a period. Next is the title of the book, also followed by a period.

Then MLA requires publication information. This includes the city of publication followed by a colon, the name of the publisher followed by a comma, and the date of publication followed by a period. The single author citation would look like the first entry on this Works Cited page.

Glossary

accurate - free of errors. Something with errors is inaccurate.

contradict - to say the opposite of a statement.

database - a large collection of information.

deliberate - planned or thought out carefully.

evaluate - to determine the meaning or importance of something.

exaggerate - to make something seem larger or greater than it is.

expel - to force out.

Internet - a way to let computers share information with other computer networks around the world.

manuscript - a book or article written by hand or typed before being published.

memoir - a written account of a person's experiences.

parenthetical - a phrase or note enclosed by two curved marks ( ) to separate it from the surrounding text.

periodical - an item that is published at a fixed period of time.

prejudice - an often negative opinion formed without knowing all the facts.

skeptical - having an attitude of doubt or disbelieving.

survey - a method of measuring opinion by talking to many different people.

Saying It

antithesis - an-TIH-thuh-suhs
bias - BEYE-uhs
exaggerate - ihg-ZA-juh-rayt
memoirs - MEHM-wahrs
parenthetical - pehr-uhn-THEH-tih-kuhl
plagiarism - PLAY-juh-rih-zuhm
thesis - THEE-suhs

Web Sites

To learn more about primary and secondary sources, visit ABDO Publishing Company on the World Wide Web at **www.abdopub.com**. Web sites about sources are featured on our Book Links page. These links are routinely monitored and updated to provide the most current information available.

Index